DESERT LIFE

DESERT LIFE

PHOTOGRAPHED BY
FRANK GREENAWAY

WRITTEN BY
BARBARA TAYLOR

DK PUBLISHING, INC.

DK

A DK PUBLISHING BOOK

www.dk.com

Project editor Christiane Gunzi **Art editor** Val Wright
Editorial assistant Deborah Murrell **Designer** Julie Staniland
Design assistant Nicola Rawson
Production Louise Barratt
Illustrations Nick Hall, Nick Hewetson, Dan Wright
Additional editorial assistance Jill Somerscales
Managing editor Sophie Mitchell
Managing art editor Miranda Kennedy

Consultants
Barry Clarke, Andy Currant,
Theresa Greenaway, Paul Hillyard, Edward Wade

Endpapers photographed by J.A.L. Cooke,
Oxford Scientific Films Ltd.

First American Edition, 1992
First Paperback Edition, 1998
4 6 8 10 9 7 5 3

Published in the United States by
DK Publishing, Inc., 95 Madison Avenue, New York, New York 10016.

Library of Congress Cataloging-in-Publication Data
Taylor, Barbara, 1954–
Desert life/by Barbara Taylor. – 1st American ed.
p. cm. – (Look closer)
Includes index.
Summary: Examines the variety of life found in the desert,
including the Greek tortoise, desert scorpion, and jewel wasp.
ISBN 0-7894-2969-1
1. Desert fauna – Juvenile literature. 2. Desert plants – Juvenile literature. (1. Desert animals.)
I. Title. II. Series: Taylor, Barbara, 1954-
Look closer.
QL 116.T39 1992
574.909'54-dc20

Color reproduction by Colourscan, Singapore
Printed and bound in China by L.Rex Printing Co., Ltd.

CONTENTS

Look for us, and we will show you the size of every animal and plant that you read about in this book.

LIFE IN A DESERT

THE HOT DAYS AND COLD NIGHTS in the desert provide a harsh habitat for wildlife. Very little rain falls, and sometimes there is no rain at all for several years. The desert sands often seem lifeless. But look under a stone, or below the surface of the sand, and you will find all kinds of animals hiding from the heat of the sun. Insects, reptiles, birds, and mammals have all adapted to the desert conditions. Many plants and animals store water in their bodies to help them survive. Some plants flower and produce seeds only after rain has fallen. Snakes, scorpions, and other desert animals can survive without food and water for long periods. They often rest during the day to escape the heat, and some even sleep through the hottest months.

The gray banded king snake
(*Lampropeltis mexicana alterna*) is 14 in. long.

The green toad
(*Bufo viridis*) is 3 1/4 in. long.

The diadem snake
(*Spalaerosophis diadema cliffordi*) is 15 in. long.

The ground beetle
(*Thermophilum sexmaculatam*) is 1 1/2 in. long

The locust nymph
(*Locustidae* family) is 1 1/4 in. long.

This cactus
(Mammillaria magnimamma)
is 3 1/2 in. wide.

The tortoise's
(Testudo graeca)
shell is 2 1/4 in. long.

This cactus
(Trichocereus)
is 6 in. high.

This cactus
(Mammillaria hahniana)
is 3 3/4 in. high.

The gerbil's
(Meriones unguiculatus)
body is 3 1/4 in. long.

This cactus's
(Mammillaria longiflora) blossom
is 1 in. long.

The scorpion
(Androctonus amoreuxi) is
3 in. long.

The sandfish
(Scincus mitranus) is
5 3/4 in. long.

The jewel wasp
(Ampulex compressa)
is 1 in. long.

SLOW COACH

TORTOISES USE UP VERY little energy in getting around, so they can survive long periods in the desert without food or drink. During the hottest months, they sometimes estivate (sleep). Tortoises feed on dead animals, dung, and any plants which emerge after a rainstorm. These reptiles are related to lizards, but unlike their cousins, tortoises are too slow to catch prey or run from enemies. In times of danger, the tortoise pulls its head back inside its shell for protection. Females lay eggs in a hole in the sand. The young tortoises break out of their shells by using the horny tooth on their snouts. They have to fend for themselves as soon as they hatch, and many are attacked and killed by birds of prey.

GUESS WHAT?
Many tortoises live for more than 100 years, and sometimes they live to be 200 years old!

ARMOR PLATING
The tortoise's shell is made up of about 60 bony plates which are joined together to form a protective shield for the body. On top of the bony plates are large, horny scales called scutes, which make the shell very strong. The top part of the shell, called the carapace, is connected to the backbone and ribs, as well as to the lower part of the shell, called the plastron.

Mottled colors on the outside of the shell help camouflage the tortoise.

TOOTHLESS JAWS

Tortoises have no teeth. Instead, their jaws have a hard, horny rim that is strong enough to bite off pieces of plants. The tortoise cannot chew its food as we can, so it must bite off pieces small enough to swallow whole.

SCALY SKIN

The tortoise's body is too large and clumsy to avoid rocks and thorny desert plants, so its skin is covered with leathery scales to protect it. This also prevents it from losing too much moisture. The scales on the legs are very large, and have a bony center.

Scientists can tell roughly how old a tortoise is by studying the growth rings on the scutes.

The high, domed shell makes it hard for an enemy to fit the tortoise inside its jaws and crush it.

The long neck stretches out from the shell to reach for plants

A ridge of small scales helps protect the eyes.

There are two nostrils on the tip of the snout. A tortoise's sense of smell is excellent.

Extra-tough scales on legs protect the tortoise from sand and rock.

Very short toes with long claws grip surfaces and pull the tortoise along.

DUNE DIVER

LYING JUST BELOW the surface of the desert, the sandfish is well protected from the heat of the sun and from enemies, such as birds and snakes. This unusual creature belongs to a group of lizards called skinks. It hunts for beetles and other insects, and travels over the sand dunes by moving its body from side to side, sort of like a fish swimming in water. The sandfish moves around mainly in the cool of the early morning and evening, and rests during the hottest hours. In the colder months, it hibernates (sleeps) under the sand. Sandfish lay two eggs which hatch after about two months. The young sandfish take almost two years to grow into adults.

GUESS WHAT?
When in danger, the sandfish can dive into loose sand and disappear from sight. Fat stored in the tail helps the lizard survive when food is hard to find.

The sandfish digs in the sand with its long snout.

The scales fit closely together and lie flat on the body so that they do not slow down the lizard.

NOSE DIGGER
The sandfish's nose is long and chisel-shaped. This helps it to push the sand aside as it moves beneath the dunes. The sandfish also uses its nose to sniff out insects and other small prey.

These strong jaws crunch up tough food, such as beetles with hard wing cases.

Fringed toes stop the feet from sinking into the soft dunes.

The sandfish's pointed tail helps it glide through the sand.

The body is long, smooth, and streamlined so that it can slip easily through the sand.

This red color of the scales matches the sands of the Arabian desert where this sandfish lives, and helps to disguise it from enemies.

The ear openings are small and low on the head. This protects the ears from sand blown by the wind.

BURIED ALIVE

When a sandfish breathes under the sand, only the underside of its body moves in and out. If the sides of the body could move, the sandfish would be able to breathe out, but not in, because the sand around it would immediately fill the space.

TRICKY TAIL

The sandfish's tail has several weak points in it that are specially designed to allow the tail to break off easily when it is grasped by a predator. The lizard will slowly grow a new tail, but the new one does not have weak points in it and cannot break off as neatly as the original tail.

HUNGRY HOPPERS

DESERT LOCUSTS are grasshoppers with short antennae (feelers). They sometimes fly together in such huge swarms that they block out sunlight. Young desert locusts are called nymphs, or hoppers. They cannot fly because their wings are not yet fully developed, so they use their long back legs to hop across the desert, sometimes forming large groups called bands. Hoppers hatch from eggs buried in the sand. Their skin is hard and does not stretch as they grow. Instead, the hoppers have to molt (shed their outer skin) from time to time. After several weeks, the hoppers develop into adult locusts with four wings. They can then take to the air.

The antennae are sensitive to touch and scent. They are jointed and can bend.

There are simple eyes at the base of the antennae that detect changes in the brightness of sunlight.

Compound eyes made up of many lenses help the locust to see up to three yards away.

WAXED JACKET
A waterproof layer of wax covers the hopper's body and helps prevent water loss in the hot, dry desert. This waxed jacket is protected by an outer layer of hard varnish. Hoppers and adult locusts never need to drink because they get all the water they need from the plants they eat.

A hard collar protects the wide part of the body called the thorax.

The hopper rubs its legs against these veins on the wings to make a chirping sound.

Hoppers gather together in bands, and hop around on the sand. The more hoppers there are, the faster they all hop.

The hard mandibles (jaws) cut and grind up food, such as grass. They work like our teeth, although they are outside the body.

These front legs hold food close to the mouth during feeding.

CHAMPION LEAPER

Young hoppers have long back legs, like adult locusts. When hoppers become adults, their legs are so powerful that they can leap up to ten times their own length. These long leaps help locusts to escape from predators, such as snakes.

COURTSHIP CALL

To attract a female for mating, a male locust makes chirping sounds. He rubs a ridge of pegs on the top part of his back leg against stiff veins on the front wing. Even hoppers have these special ridges on their legs.

GUESS WHAT?

A swarm of locusts can contain millions of individuals. Adult locusts often fly for thousands of miles, and they devastate huge areas of crops when they land to eat.

Each time the hopper molts, its wings grow bigger.

The long back legs have strong muscles for leaping.

ON THE MARCH

Large bands of hoppers sometimes carpet the desert sands for several square miles. They rest during the heat of the day and usually feed in the cool of the morning and evening. A band of hoppers may travel as far as a mile in a day.

A special ridge of pegs on each leg is used for making chirping sounds.

The abdomen has many segments so it can bend.

Sharp spines on each leg deter snakes from attacking. They also help the hopper to grip onto plant stems.

When this female hopper becomes an adult, she will use the end of her abdomen to dig a hole in the sand for her eggs.

The tough, hard feet with hooks for holding on to rocks and plants.

STING IN THE TAIL

THE SCORPION IS ONE of the most dangerous creatures in the desert. This desert scorpion can kill a human with its poisonous sting, although it usually only stings to protect itself and to kill its prey. Scorpions are well suited to life in the dry desert because they can go without water for several months. They can also survive for more than a year without eating any food. Scorpions are active mainly at night. During the day, they hide away in burrows or under stones, where it is cool and damp. The female gives birth to several young, which look like tiny versions of their parents. When the young have molted once, they leave their mother and go off to fend for themselves. Young scorpions take about a year to develop into adults.

The tail is actually a narrow section of the abdomen.

Poison is produced in two glands inside the swollen part of the stinger.

The scorpion arches its tail over its head and injects poison through the sharp tip of the sting. The poison paralyzes the victim so it cannot move.

The tip of the stinger is long and sharp for piercing the victim's skin.

Joints between the segments of the tail allow it to bend easily.

HAIRY LEGS
Stiff hairs on the scorpion's legs detect tiny vibrations (movements) in the air. The time it takes for the vibrations to travel from the front legs to the back legs helps the scorpion to assess the position of its food, a mate, or an enemy.

The sandy coloring is a good disguise when the scorpion moves around during the day.

Hairs on the legs detect the movements of other creatures.

GUESS WHAT?
Sometimes the female scorpion kills and eats the male scorpion after they have mated.

DEADLY INJECTION
Most scorpions are harmless to people, and their stings are no more dangerous than a wasp's sting. But the venom (poison) from the sting of this scorpion destroys the nerves in the victim's body and can kill a person in a few hours.

JOINTED JAWS
Scorpions feed on insects, centipedes, spiders, and small lizards. Strong, jointed jaws outside the mouth tear food into pieces and crush it into a soft pulp. Special fluids from the stomach help digest the food. The scorpion then sucks up the juices from its victim's body into its very small mouth.

Scorpions have four pairs of eyes, but they cannot see well. Because their eyes are small and simple, they find their food mainly by touch and smell.

Jointed jaws tear up food into small pieces.

CLAWED HANDS
The scorpion has two special legs called pedipalps that have strong pincers on the ends that grab and hold food. Male and female scorpions also hold each other by their pincers during their courtship dance.

Pedipalps have strong pincers for catching food.

SPINY ARMOR

CACTUSES CAN SURVIVE with very little water, and some kinds can live for years without any water at all. Cactus roots spread out near the surface so that they can soak up moisture from dew or brief rainstorms. Most plants lose water through tiny breathing holes in their leaves and stems. But cactuses have developed spines rather than leaves, and they have fewer holes in their stems, so less water can escape. Inside the stem, there are cells that store water like a sponge. New cactuses grow from branches, called offsets, which sprout near the base of the parent cactus. They also grow from seeds that develop if one cactus flower receives pollen from another of the same kind.

GUESS WHAT?
These small, round cactuses only grow to be about two inches high. But the tall one can grow up to a yard high if the conditions are right.

PRICKLY SPINES
The tough, sharp spines protect the cactus in many ways. They help to shade the stem and collect dew in the early morning. The dew runs down to the soil, where the roots absorb it. The spines also trap a layer of air around the plant so less moisture is blown away by the wind. Animals that try to eat the cactus are soon discouraged by the prickly spines.

Fine hairs shield the stem against strong sunlight.

RARE BLOOMS
These brightly colored cactus flowers attract insects, such as bees and beetles. The insects feed on the flowers' nectar and carry pollen from one flower to another. When a cactus flower opens, lots of precious water escapes from the petals. For this reason, cactuses usually flower for only a few days each year.

In the center of the flower there are bags of yellow pollen.

The hooks on the spines of these cactuses give them the popular name of fishhook cactus.

White spines reflect sunlight away from the cactus.

These ribs can expand to store water.

ACCORDION STEM

The stems of cactuses like this one are folded into pleats that expand and contract like an accordion. This helps the cactus to store as much water as possible when it rains. The stems contain up to 90 percent water. Without its pleats, the cactus would split open.

The stem's green color is due to chlorophyll, a substance that the plant uses to convert sunlight to food.

The stem has a thick, waxy surface that prevents water from escaping.

Spines grow out of small side branches called areoles.

SPIKY SPOKES

Cactuses have very short side branches called areoles. The spines grow out of the areoles in clusters like the spokes of a wheel, so that they cast as much shade as possible. There are extra spines on the top of the cactus to protect the delicate growing tip.

Extra spines on the top of the plant

JUMPING GERBILS

THESE AGILE GERBILS jump and scurry about in the desert in the cool of the night. During the day, they usually hide away from the dry heat in burrows underground. Gerbils never drink. They get all the water they need from their food. At night, when gerbils come out for food, the seeds they find are dampened by the dew. Gerbils take their food back to their burrow to eat. These seeds take in more moisture from the damp air in the burrow. The female Mongolian gerbil visits another burrow to mate with a male, but returns to the safety of her own burrow to give birth to her young. The young are born with fur, and their eyes are closed. Like other mammals, they feed on their mother's milk for the first few weeks. The adult males in the burrow help to look after the young until they are old enough to fend for themselves.

The gerbil's large eyes can see in the dark and can spot danger in time for it to leap away quickly.

Gerbils hold food in their front paws while they eat it.

Pale, sandy-colored fur camouflages the gerbil against the desert sand.

Large ears allow the gerbil to hear enemies, such as foxes and snakes.

FOOD STORES

Mongolian gerbils eat the seeds of desert plants. These plants flower and produce seeds only after brief rainstorms. When there is plenty of food available, gerbils store seeds in their burrows. Special pouches in their cheeks help them carry many seeds at once. They can eat these later when food is hard to find.

The special pouches in the cheeks stretch so the gerbil can carry lots of food in its mouth.

Large back feet help the gerbil to stand upright so it can search for enemies.

TRICKY TAIL

This gerbil's beige-colored coat matches the color of the sand where it lives. If it comes out during the day, predators such as birds and foxes cannot see it easily. A tuft of darker fur on the end of the tail acts as a decoy, so that if an enemy sees the gerbil at all, it will attack its tail. The tail can break off completely if this happens, but it cannot grow back again.

GUESS WHAT?
Gerbils are great hoarders of food. One Mongolian gerbil was found with 44 lbs. of seeds stored in its burrow.

There is a dark tuft on the end of the tail to attract enemies away from the animal's head.

KANGAROO HOP

Gerbils have fur on the undersides of their feet to protect them from the hot desert sand. They also can make huge leaps on their long back legs so their feet do not have to touch the sand very often. The gerbil uses its long tail for balance and to change direction as it bounds along like a tiny kangaroo.

Powerful back legs launch the gerbil up and forward through the air.

Large ears allow the gerbil to hear enemies, such as foxes and snakes.

The white fur on the belly reflects heat to help the gerbil keep cool.

Long, sensitive whiskers help the gerbil feel its way in the dark and underground.

Sturdy front legs support the weight of the gerbil's body on landing.

SCALY SLITHERERS

BECAUSE OF THEIR watertight skin, snakes survive well in the desert. Like other reptiles, they need the heat of the sun to warm their bodies and give them the energy to move. Snakes can survive for a long time without eating. This is useful in the desert where their food of birds, small mammals, and reptiles is often hard to find. King snakes do not see or hear well; they rely mainly on their senses of smell and taste to find food and escape enemies. Diadem snakes have better eyesight, and can spot their prey if it is moving. Female snakes lay soft-shelled eggs under stones or below the surface of the sand, where it is warm and damp, then they leave them. As soon as the eggs have hatched, the young snakes can fend for themselves and find prey, such as small lizards.

STRETCHY SKIN

The king snake's skin expands when the snake swallows a meal larger than itself. Like other snakes, it molts as it grows. About a week before it molts, the snake goes blind and the eyes look blue and cloudy. They clear again about two days before the snake molts.

The skin is made up of thick, horny scales, that overlap each other. The skin stretches easily between the scales.

The coloring and pattern of the king snake is similar to the poisonous coral snake's. Enemies may think the king snake is poisonous, too.

FORKED TONGUE

A snake's forked tongue picks up scent particles from the air and carries them to a special part of the mouth called the Jacobson's organ. The snake builds up a picture of its surroundings based on different scents. This helps it to track down food and avoid enemies. This special sense helps to make up for the snake's weak hearing and eyesight.

GUESS WHAT?

Snakes do not have external ears, so they do not hear sounds which travel through the air, as we do. Instead, snakes are able to pick up vibrations through the ground.

BUILT FOR SPEED

The diadem snake is streamlined for speed, so it can move quickly and quietly to escape from enemies and catch its prey. Snakes wriggle along in a series of S-shaped curves. The scales on the underside grip the sand so the snake does not slip.

The eyes cannot see an object clearly unless it is moving.

The tongue flicks out even when the mouth is shut. The snake uses its tongue to smell, as well as to taste and touch things.

The colors and patterns on this diadem snake's scales match the surroundings and help to hide it from enemies.

There are no eyelids, so the eyes cannot close. Instead, they are covered by a protective transparent scale.

The mouth can open very wide because the jaws are loosely joined to the skull by special hingelike bones.

Nostrils allow the snake to smell the air.

SPEEDY SPRINTER

THIS GROUND BEETLE is as fierce a hunter as it looks, chasing after other insects and spiders on its long legs. It cannot fly because its wings are stuck together, but it can run very fast and has good eyesight for spotting prey. Food is often scarce in the desert, but ground beetles can survive for months without eating. There are four stages in a beetle's life. First, the female lays eggs, which hatch into larvae (grubs). Each larva molts three times as it grows. Eventually the larva becomes a pupa, and its whole body changes shape until it finally turns into an adult beetle. This kind of ground beetle is sometimes called a domino beetle because of the white spots on its black body. The bold pattern warns enemies not to attack. If they do, the beetle may spray them with a special chemical that burns.

BODY ON STILTS

The ground beetle has three pairs of long, slender legs, all about the same size. They help the beetle to run fast when chasing prey or escaping from enemies. They also hold the beetle's body high above the hot desert sand.

A very large head allows space for the beetle's oversized jaw muscles.

Large compound eyes have many separate lenses. These give the beetle the keen eyesight it needs for hunting.

The long antennae (feelers) are joined to the side of the head. They pick up vibrations and scents from the air.

The large, strong mandibles are perfect for chopping up food, such as other insects and their larvae.

Hairs line its body and legs.

Hooks on its legs and feet help the beetle to grip onto sand and rocks without slipping.

JAGGED JAWS

The ground beetle grabs its prey with its pointed, toothed jaws. Then it uses its other mouthparts to tear the food into pieces. Once an animal is caught, it has little chance of escape.

Jointed legs allow the beetle to move easily and nimbly in its desert home.

HAIRY LEGS

Tiny hairs on the legs and body are sensitive to vibrations (movements) in the air. This helps the beetle to detect enemies and search for food or a mate.

GUESS WHAT?

Adult ground beetles can live for several years. This one is at least six years old.

OUTSIDE SKELETON

Like all insects, the ground beetle has an outer skeleton called an exoskeleton. It is made of a hard substance called chitin. This adult beetle has now reached its full size and will not molt again.

Rows of dots along the wing cases help scientists to tell this beetle apart from other kinds.

The wing cases are stuck together to form a protective shield.

The beetle's hard exoskeleton protects the fragile body.

This ground beetle can squirt a jet of nasty burning chemicals from the rear end of its body to deter enemies.

The body is flexible between each segment and it can bend easily.

WARTY TOAD

DURING THE DAY, the green toad hides from the heat of the sun under a rock or in the sand, where it is cool. The toad comes out to feed at night, using its long, sticky tongue to catch ants and other small insects. Toads can survive well in hot, dry areas because they never need to drink. They absorb moisture from food and through their skin instead. Green toads have small bumps on their skin that produce a slimy mucus to keep them moist. There are also large warts all over the body containing poison. This poison protects the toad from predators. Green toads that live in hot, dry, desert areas only breed after a rainstorm because, like other amphibians, they need to lay their eggs in pools of water. The eggs develop into tadpoles, and after about a year they become fully grown toads.

TOAD TALK
Toads hear well. They have a flat, round eardrum on each side of the head, just below the poison gland. Toads make many different kinds of sounds to scare off enemies and to communicate with each other when they are looking for a mate.

Green toads have a third eyelid that slides across the eye for protection when they are under soil or sand.

The pupil in the middle of each eyeball can close to a slit in really bright sunlight.

TOOTHLESS WONDER
The toad has no teeth and swallows its food whole. Each time it swallows, its eyeballs sink down toward the mouth to help force food down the throat.

MOUTH BREATHER
To pump air in and out of its lungs, the toad pushes the lower part of its mouth up and down and moves its throat muscles in and out. The toad can also breathe through its moist skin.

Green toads can breathe through their skin.

GUESS WHAT?
An adult female green toad often lays more than 10,000 eggs at one time.

Each foot has fingers that the toad uses to wipe dirt off its food.

There is a round, flat eardrum on each side of the head called a tympanum. These pick up vibrations in the air.

The large lump behind the eye is a poison gland called the paratoid gland.

These large knobbly warts produce poison.

POISONOUS WARTS

The brightly colored patterns on the toad's skin act as a disguise and also warn enemies that it is poisonous. Predators soon learn to leave the toad alone. The poisons are produced in a special gland behind the eye and also in the large warts all over the skin.

Bright colors and patterns deter enemies.

DESERT DAZZLER

LIKE SEVERAL OTHER WASPS, the dazzling jewel wasp is a solitary creature. It does not form large colonies like the familiar black-and-yellow-striped wasps that buzz around us in the summer. Adult jewel wasps feed on the sweet nectar in flowers, but their larvae, or grubs, are parasites (animals that live off another living creature). The female wasp stings a cockroach to paralyze it so that it cannot move. Then she drags it into a hole in the sand, and lays a single egg on it. The cockroach eventually dies, but it stays fresh for weeks because the poison in the sting contains an antiseptic to prevent the flesh from rotting. The larva hatches from the egg about three days later. It has no legs, because it feeds on the cockroach and does not need to search for additional food. When it has eaten enough, it turns into a pupa, and about three weeks later emerges as an adult wasp.

BUG EYES

Huge compound eyes, made up of many separate lenses, provide the jewel wasp with excellent eyesight. The eyes are set on each side of the head, which can swivel freely. This means the wasp can look all around for enemies, such as lizards, or cockroaches for its young to feed on.

The two pairs of wings hook together during flight, and fold back across the body when not in use.

Close up, you can see tiny hairs on the insect's body. These help absorb heat, which the wasp needs in order to stay active.

These orange-colored legs warn enemies that the wasp is poisonous.

Hooks grip the defeated cockroach.

The antennae pick up scents in the air and help the wasp find its prey.

GUESS WHAT?

The jewel wasp's sting developed over thousands of years from the egg-laying tube, so only females are capable of stinging.

Long legs for running fast when hunting or escaping from enemies.

STRONG GRIP

The female jewel wasp digs a hole for her egg by moving grains of sand with her strong jaws and kicking away loose sand with her legs. She also grips her cockroach victim firmly in her jaws while injecting venom into its body from the sting on the tip of her abdomen. Adult jewel wasps feed on nectar, so they use their jaws mainly when preparing a home for their young.

A small cockroach like this one is easy prey. Sometimes a wasp will choose a cockroach almost twice its own size.

GLOSSARY

Abdomen *the rear part of the body*
Aestivate *to rest or sleep during the hot months of the year*
Amphibian *an animal such as a frog, which lives both on land and in water*
Antennae *a pair of feelers*
Camouflage *the colors or patterns of an animal that match its background*
Exoskeleton *a tough covering on the body, made of a substance called chitin*
Larva *the young, grublike stage of an animal such as an insect*
Mandibles *jaws*

Mammal *a warm-blooded animal such as a mouse or rabbit*
Molt *to shed the skin or exoskeleton*
Mucus *a slimy, often poisonous substance that certain animals produce*
Pupa *the resting stage between a larva and an adult insect*
Reptile *a cold-blooded animal such as a turtle or snake*
Thorax *the middle part of the body, containing the heart and lungs*
Vibrations *tiny movements in air, in water, or underground*